To: _____

From: _____

BEACH WISDOM

Published by Sellers Publishing, Inc.
Text and illustrations copyright © 2012 Sandy Gingras
All rights reserved.

Sellers Publishing, Inc.
161 John Roberts Road, South Portland, Maine 04106
Visit our Web site: www.sellerspublishing.com
E-mail: rsp@rsvp.com

ISBN 13: 978-1-4162-0646-0

10 9 8 7 6 5 4 3 2

Printed and bound in China.

BEACH WISDOM

by Sandy Gingras

SELLERS
PUBLISHING

The beach is full of wisdom. There's a lesson in that wave you have to dive under, and in the wave that lifts you up. There's counsel in that sudden storm. There's truth in the tide that turns. There's good advice everywhere at the beach, if we pay attention...

A Little bikini
is no match for
a big wave.

Sometimes you have to
go back and forth a Lot

to get anywhere.

Summer is always
the shortest
season

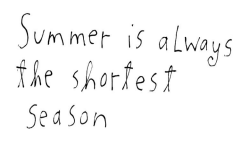

(no matter what
the calendar says).

Sometimes you get sand in your pants.

Naps happen.

An outside shower
makes you feel
cLeaner than an
inside shower.

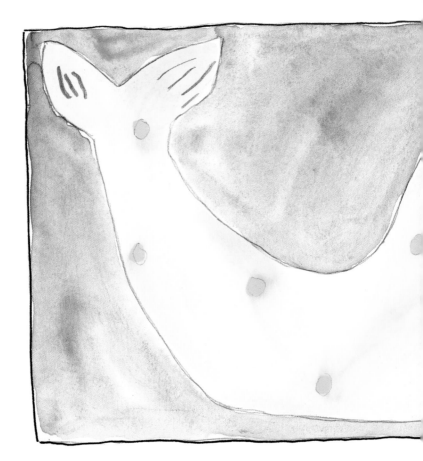

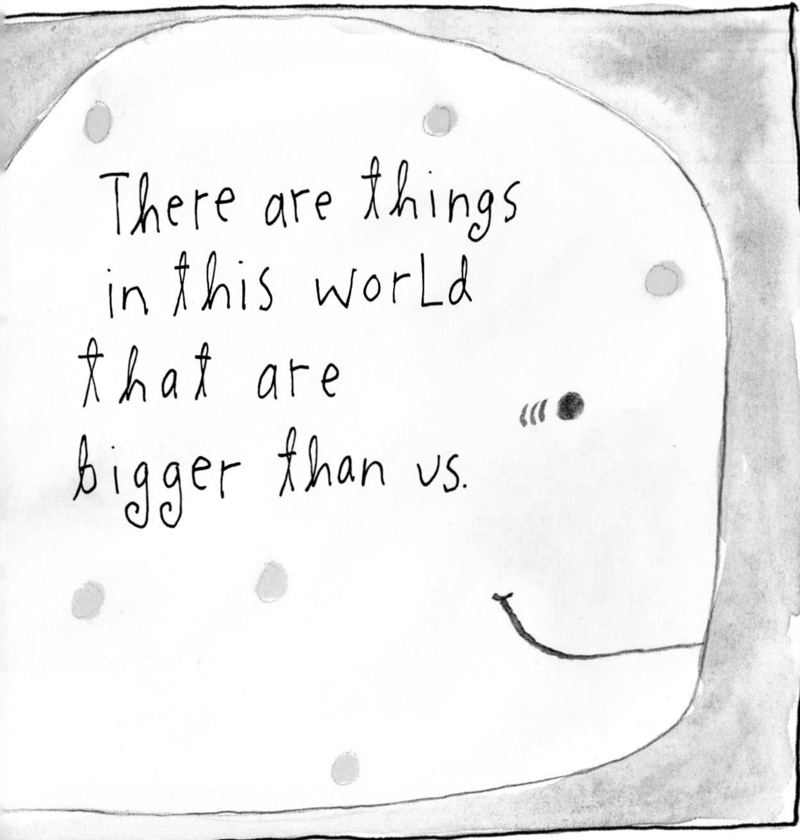

There are things in this world that are bigger than us.

Sometimes,
you wipe out.

Company...

is coming

Everyone wants a turn in the captain's chair.

Don't put the crab bait next to the ice cream.

Jump

for joy.

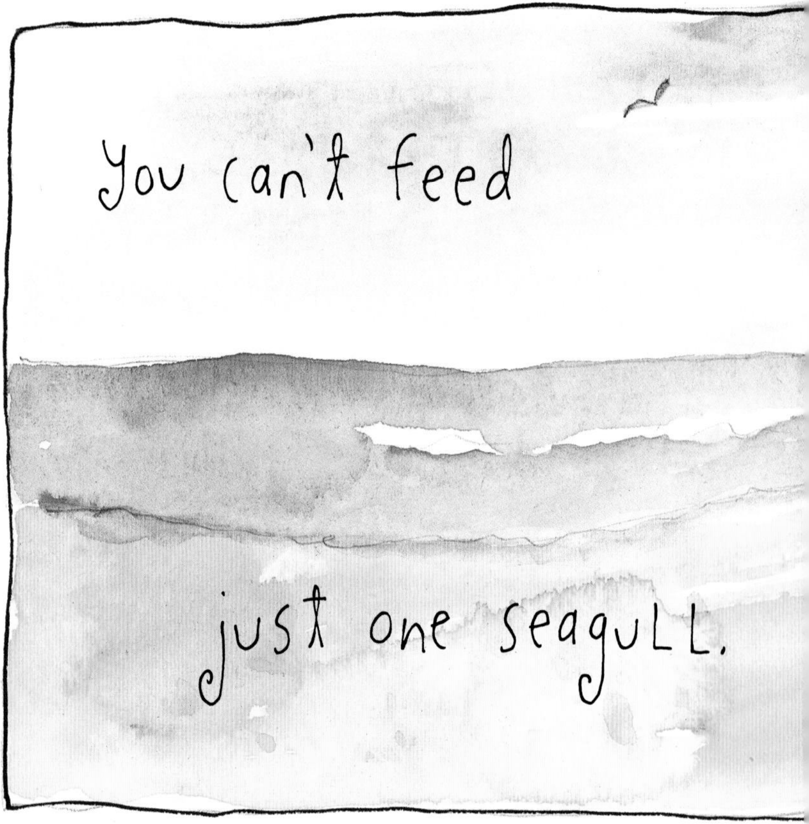
You can't feed
just one seagull.

Rainy days make you appreciate sunny days.

There's a Lot of Life

in a Little tidaL pooL.

You're never too old
to boogie.

Stop whatever you're doing

to watch the sunset

is not necessariLy
the best.

when it storms.

no working during drinking hours
SeeDy's DIVE BAR
Go where the LocaLs go.

Don't dig a hole deeper than you.

Pedal hard,
glide,
pedal hard,
glide,
pedal hard...

Another wave

Go to the place
that
makes
the
home-made donuts

Crabs are

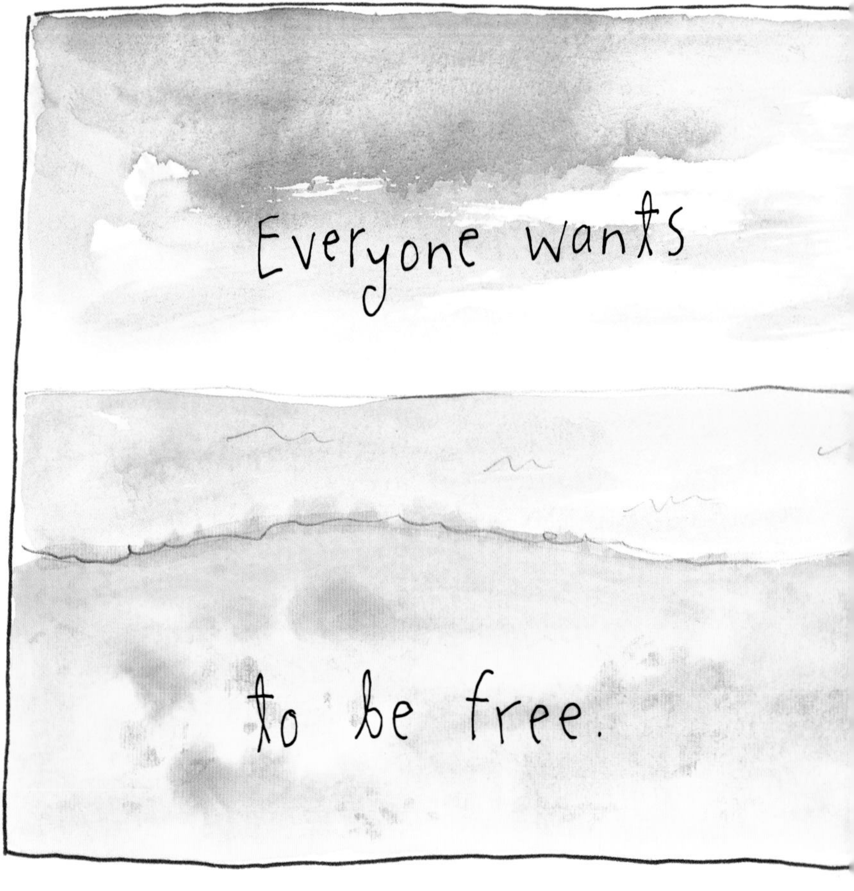
Everyone wants
to be free.

You don't need as much as you think you do.

Re-apply